LorD,
I NEED AN
ANSWER

LORD, I NEED AN ANSWER

Story Devotions for Girls

BETTY WESTROM SKOLD

AUGSBURG Publishing House • Minneapolis

LORD, I NEED AN ANSWER

Copyright © 1982 Augsburg Publishing House

Library of Congress Catalog Card No. 81-052279

International Standard Book No. 0-8066-1911-2

Scripture quotations unless otherwise noted are from the Revised
Standard Version of the Bible, copyright 1946, 1952, and 1971
by the Division of Christian Education of the National Council
of Churches.

Illustrations: Koechel/Peterson Design

MANUFACTURED IN THE UNITED STATES OF AMERICA

This book is for Jenny and Kristen and Carly,
and for every girl who has ever made
her granny happy and proud.

Contents

About This Book

Problems, problems. Problem solving can be like a tough riddle. No matter how hard you try, you just can't figure out the right answer. Until a problem is solved, the whole world can look like it's painted the wrong color.

If you want to learn something about problem solving, just watch a squirrel at a bird feeder. People buy all kinds of devices to keep squirrels away from the cracked corn or the sunflower seeds that are meant for the birds. But somehow that squirrel finds a way. He may tremble a lot. He may have to stretch his body until it almost pulls apart. He may fall to the ground and fail a hundred times, but he doesn't give up on himself. That squirrel has a stubborn faith that he'll find the answer. He's convinced he's entitled to what's in that feeder.

In this book are stories that all have to do with problems—mostly problems that come up in everyday living for girls your age. These stories don't crank out any magic solutions, but I'm hoping they'll encourage you to hang in there, like that squirrel, and keep looking for answers. Have a stubborn faith that, with the help of God and of other friends who care about you, you will have success in problem solving.

These stories are passed along to you with love. I'm hoping the girls in them have some of the feelings that you have. While the stories might not all be about your particular problems, read them anyway. Maybe you can find an idea to share with a friend.

Each story begins with a question and ends with a prayer—not a bad pattern for anybody who wants to live a happy life.

Because these are stories about real problems, I needed the help of real people in order to write them—mostly girls your age. Special thank-yous go to Nancy Moersch, Amy Domstrand, Gina Voller, Holly Foster, Andrea and Nicole Lord, Jenny Bren, Nikki McComb, Jenny Magnuson, Dina DuPont, Heidi Huselid, and Tanya Neisen.

I'm also grateful to my own daughter, Carol Skold Uecker, and to three other young mothers, Corrine Lindstrom, Sandy Neisen, and Kathy Huselid. Thanks, too, to my husband, Bill, for his unfailing encouragement.

Thanks in Action

Why do I always have to write thank-you notes at Christmas and birthday times? It's so hard to know what to say, and besides, don't they kind of know I like the presents?

"You OK, Mom?"

It worried Robin when she came into the kitchen and saw her mother just sitting there with the phone held loosely in her hand, looking at nothing. Mom folded in her upper lip, her eyes swimming with tears.

"No, Robin," she shook her head. "I'm not all right, but don't worry about me. I will be. It's Aunt Libby."

"Aunt Libby? You mean there's bad news about Aunt Libby?"

"She's had a stroke, Robin. Aunt Libby has lost the use of her right hand and arm."

"You mean forever?"

"That's hard to say, but maybe forever."

"But that can't be. That means there won't be any more—" Robin stopped, her face reddening a little under the freckles.

"You were going to say, 'There won't be any more mittens.' Don't be embarrassed, Robin. I'm sure Aunt Libby would understand."

"It's just that when I think of Aunt Libby, I always think about mittens. To tell the truth I was kind of expecting the box to come. That was pretty grabby of me, right?"

Every year, as regularly as Christmas itself, Aunt Libby's package had always arrived. The outside wrapping was always a brown grocery bag that had been cut open along the seams. Inside the big box were the small packages, one for Robin and one each for her brothers, Chad and Rusty. They were wrapped in white tissue paper, stuck together with little pictures of Santa Claus or toy soldiers or candy canes. And each small package contained this year's pair of mittens. You could depend on it.

Once Aunt Libby had explained her reasons for the mittens. "By the time I get home from work at the factory, I'm too tired to have an original idea about presents, so I just sit down and knit mittens one more time. I figure warm mittens are something that you'll always need."

When they were little, there was always a string connecting the two mittens. The string reached down through the coat sleeves to keep the two mittens together so they wouldn't get lost so easily.

When Robin got a little older, Aunt Libby was afraid it might look too babyish to include the string, even though there was still danger of losing them. That year there were three mittens in her package, two for the right hand and one for the left. A note pinned to them explained Aunt Libby's reason.

"Hi. I figure there's a 50-50 chance that the right-hand mitten will be the one that gets lost. If it turns out I guessed wrong, just let me know, and I'll get back to work."

And before the Christmas wrappings had even been carried down the apartment house hall to the trash compactor, Mom began talking about writing the thank-you notes. Robin did like the mittens. They were bright and warm, and they were so thick they didn't wear out until the next Christmas. It was just that writing the notes was such a bother.

"Mom, she knows we like them."

"How does she know if you don't tell her so?"

"Well, when we see her, we have them on."

"I'm not going to argue with you about it, Robin. A present deserves a thank-you, and those new mittens will not be worn until Aunt Libby has been thanked."

And so, every year, the note was written.

Robin grew sober at the thought. "All those notes that I wrote to her without really thinking about it —and now it's too late."

"Too late?"

"Well, yes," Robin said. "I guess this is the end of it. No more mittens."

"I would say you're not a bit too late. It's never too late to learn how to really thank somebody."

"But she'd just feel bad, Mom, if I wrote to her now. She'd just remember how she can't make mittens anymore."

15

"Every year Aunt Libby has given something to you. Maybe the time has finally come when you can give her something."

"You mean make her a present?" Robin pondered for a moment. "How would it be if I made a vase by covering a bottle with scraps of masking tape and rubbing it with shoe polish? We made some in craft class."

"I'll bet she'd like that. But she'd really love it if we'd drive over to Higginstown so you could deliver it in person. She's home from the hospital, and she probably gets pretty lonesome when she can't go off to work."

Aunt Libby looked pretty much like herself when she came to the door—broad-shouldered, a little overweight, her brown hair done in a short, no-nonsense haircut. Robin tried not to stare at her right hand, which hung down kind of limply at her side.

"Kay! Robin! How great of you to come! I'm not too good at shaking hands right now, but I can still manage a pretty good hug."

As Aunt Libby pulled her up close with her strong left arm, Robin felt glad that she had come.

Then Robin handed her the vase, filled with a few Christmas greens.

"I made it for you, Aunt Libby. It got lumpy in a couple of places, but—"

"Lumpy? What do you mean lumpy? It's perfectly beautiful, Robin. Thank you. I just love it. Thank you."

Later, when Aunt Libby offered them orange juice, Robin said, "Let me do it, Aunt Libby. I'll pour the juice."

"Not a chance," her aunt said with a grin. "This

left hand will never get clever if I get too much help."

While Aunt Libby was in the kitchen, Robin picked up her thick "memory book" from the coffee table. Robin remembered that it was filled with all kinds of interesting stuff, little things Aunt Libby had pasted in there to remind herself of things she'd done. There was an old snapshot of Robin's mother when she was a little girl, holding up a great big fish. There was a high school graduation announcement and a little shriveled-up flower with a faded ribbon on it. And in the back part of the book Robin found one of her own thank-you notes, the first one she had ever written, with a funny drawing of a big pair of mittens.

"I wouldn't part with that note for anything, Robin," Aunt Libby said, handing her a glass. "How I've enjoyed your notes!"

"Well, you know, it was really Mom who told us to write them."

Aunt Libby grinned at Robin's confession. "Of course. It's your Mom's job to teach you good habits. One good habit is to say 'thank you' for things."

"I suppose that's right." Robin hadn't thought about it before, but she agreed.

"When you were small and you wrote that first little unreadable note to me, I smiled because I knew that your Mom was helping your hands to form the letters."

Robin's mother nodded. "I wanted to know that when you got bigger, and I could take my hand away, you would still keep the good habit of gratefulness."

"You know, Robin," Aunt Libby said, "it's like

that string I used to crochet connecting the mittens."

"The string?" Robin looked puzzled.

"Yes. You see, there is a connection between the words *thank you* and a grateful heart—or at least there should be. It's important that they don't get separated from each other and lost."

"I was always just being polite, Aunt Libby, but now I'm finally thinking about you and all those mittens. I guess I'm starting to understand what kind of person would go to all that work for me."

"That's beautiful, Robin. When you made me that vase it was even better than a thank-you note. It's like the woman in the Bible story who poured all of her perfume over Jesus' feet. You found a way of acting out your love and gratitude."

Robin nodded, then smiled. "And it's a neat feeling, Aunt Libby. It's really a neat feeling."

> Let us come into his presence with thanksgiving.
>
> Psalm 95:2a

Sometimes, Lord, I'm in such a rush to grab at a gift I don't even bother to look at the giver. I do that with gifts from people who love me, and even with gifts from you. I write thank-you notes because I have to, and I say prayers of thanksgiving because I know I should, but teach me to be thankful, really thankful. Amen

God Doesn't Seem to Hear Me

Every time I'm really worried or I want something special, somebody tells me, "Pray about it," but that doesn't always work. Three times lately I tried that, and nothing happened. Why should I keep on trying?

"Was that the clock striking? It's midnight! Time to go!" There was genuine panic in Erica's voice. Her eyes widened, and she covered her mouth with one hand, a hand glittering with rings from the gumball machine. She whirled in front of the mirror, clutching at the flowered beach towel which she had wrapped around her jeans.

"Hey, small person, what are you playing this time?"

Erica stopped in her tracks and looked up into the mocking face of her big brother, Paul.

"It's nothing to laugh about, Paul. There are try-outs for the summer recreation play *Cinderella*. I'm practicing."

"And you're trying out for the Cinderella part, and you want it so bad you can taste it. Right?"

"Well, right, but wanting it doesn't mean it'll happen. There's even some chance the play will be called off. Mrs. Clark, the director, might not be able to do it because her husband is in the hospital."

"Well, Erica, I hope Prince Charming comes along pretty soon so you can chuck those beat-up running shoes and swoop around in glass slippers. Glass slippers have got more class."

Erica looked down at her blue and yellow running shoes. Paul was right. Not even the ugly stepsisters would go to the ball in these shoes.

Mother appeared in the doorway. "Paul, would you stop teasing your sister and carry the sprinkler around to the perennial bed?"

Erica was relieved. "He thinks it's a big joke. Mom, but I just have to get to be Cinderella."

"You really want it, don't you, Erica?"

"Oh, yes, I do. I really do want it. Mom, it would be so great. I've seen the gown for the ball scene. It's white and fluffy, with blue ribbon strung through the lace."

"Sounds beautiful."

"And I'd have my name on posters at the playground and at the library. I can just see it—Starring Erica Worthing as Cinderella."

"Well, that does have a nice ring to it."

"And besides, Shelley Blaisdell wants the part, too, and she'll be really upset if I beat her," Erica added smugly.

"You'll just have to pray about it, honey," was her mother's cheerful answer.

Erica looked doubtful. "That wouldn't work. I've tried praying about some things lately, and nothing happens."

"Like what kinds of things?"

"Well, I asked for a horse, for one thing, and nothing happened."

"And?"

"And I didn't get on student council, and we didn't get to go to Disneyland, and I prayed really hard that Grandpa wouldn't die, and it didn't do one bit of good. God doesn't seem to listen when I pray. I can't see him, so how do I know he's even there?"

"When you walk into the house and smell supper cooking, do you have to see me to know I'm there?"

"No, I just figure you must be around somewhere. Where there's the smell of meat loaf or cauliflower, there's got to be somebody in the kitchen."

"Well, that's the idea. God isn't somebody you can see, but if you keep your eyes and ears open for the things he does, you'll know he's around."

"Well, maybe he's around, but from the way my prayers get answered you wouldn't know it."

"I wonder if God suspects you've been keeping a scorecard on his performance."

"I know what you mean, but is it wrong for me to wonder why my prayers aren't getting results?"

"No, Erica, there's nothing wrong with that, I guess, but maybe you should really try to figure out the reason instead of just complaining about the service. You see yourself as Cinderella, but are you sure you haven't been trying to cast God in the role of fairy godmother?"

She thought about that. "You mean I want him to just wave a wand and make things happen?"

"Something like that, Erica. God isn't some magical creature who goes around turning pumpkins into coaches and mice into horses just because somebody makes a wish. God really cares for us and keeps track of us as persons. He can't say yes to everything. Some things just wouldn't be good for us."

"I guess it's like when you used to plop me into the cart at the supermarket, and I kept reaching for things I couldn't have."

Mother nodded. "Your eyes saw a hundred things to want. And you know, one side of me wanted to sail through the checkout line with every cream-filled cake and frosted cereal you grabbed for. It was hard for me, sometimes, putting things back on the shelf when you wanted them so much. But there were good reasons for saying no."

"You mean God loves me so much that he'd like to say yes to everything?"

"Well, maybe. It's hard to know about that. I do know that he loves me and that he sometimes has to say no to me, Erica. And more often than not I'm able to understand, a little later, that God's answer made sense. God wants some wonderful things to happen in our lives, and usually the things he wants for us are more important than the things we think we want."

"Sometimes I really want God to help me figure something out. I ask him to tell me what to do about something, but there's no answer. Isn't he supposed to be my teacher and guide? That's what we learned in Sunday school."

"Maybe it's like homework, Erica. What if every

time you think you're stuck on a math problem I just handed you the answer? Would you ever learn to figure it out for yourself?"

"I guess not."

"God knows every answer himself, Erica, and he does want you to get the answers right, but sometimes he lets you wait awhile before he shows you how to work out a problem. That way you understand its meaning better. The answer itself is sometimes less valuable than the process of putting the answer together."

"I suppose God does want me to ask for help, but maybe he wants me to get better at my own problem solving too."

"You've got the idea, Erica. And you know he told us to believe when we pray, but that's not always easy to do."

"That's for sure, Mom. Sometimes, even while I'm praying, I catch myself thinking, 'I'm pretty sure you can't do this, God, but it's worth a try.' I suppose that isn't the way to do it, but I'm just being honest. I'm really not sure he can do it."

"It's not a case of God being unable to handle it, but maybe your faith isn't big enough for your part of the job—believing. Wouldn't it be better to start out by praying for things you're sure God can do instead of by begging for a miracle?"

"I guess so. Then maybe the next time my faith would be strong enough to handle a little bigger request."

"The way in which we pray says a lot about us," Mother went on. "Sometimes I find myself asking for something that I know isn't quite right. Did that ever happen to you, honey?"

Erica looked a little uncomfortable. "I remember once when I lied to you about my math grade."

"And you prayed about it?"

"Well, yes, I prayed all right, but not a real great prayer. I prayed that you and Dad wouldn't find out what I had done."

Mother shook her head, but she was smiling a little. "We did find out, didn't we, Erica? And I guess you already know why God turned you down on that one."

"And lots of times I ask for something dumb. Like once I asked for my own TV in my room so I could always get to choose the channel."

"We all do things like that," Mom said. "We're really asking for more than our share. If giving something to me means somebody else gets less, I can see it wouldn't be right."

"I want God to answer my prayers, but then I pout when his answer is no," Erica admitted.

"And it's almost as hard when he answers, 'Wait awhile.' Right, Erica?"

"That's right. I'm not very good at waiting."

"But suppose the answer is held up because something is getting in the way. We might ask God for forgiveness while our own hearts are unforgiving."

Erica pondered for a moment, then brightened. "I see. Our hearts have to be in shape before God can take our prayers seriously. If I want the Cinderella part just so I can show off or so I can get my name on a poster or beat Shelley Blaisdell at something, God won't think I'm ready. If everybody had reasons like that for wanting a part, it wouldn't be much of a play."

"You're getting the idea. Do you suppose Cinderella found a happy ending just because she happened to have the right shoe size?"

"I guess not. Maybe it was because she was a certain kind of girl. She was kind, and she shared things. Maybe she deserved to be happy."

"God wants to write a happy ending for you, too, Erica. Maybe he wants you to have the Cinderella role, maybe not. I'm not sure, but I am sure he'd like you to be a certain kind of girl."

Mom turned to go back to her gardening. She paused in the doorway. "I think you're ready to try another prayer, Erica. Why not just tell God what you're feeling?"

Erica watched her mother go, then unwound the beach towel and let it drop to the floor. She walked slowly around the living room, deep in thought, then plopped herself down in the big chair.

"Well, here goes, Lord," she said, folding her hands and squeezing her eyes shut.

"I've been wanting the Cinderella part, God, and I thought if I pestered you about it long enough you'd give in, but now I see that isn't how you operate.

"I've been wanting the part for a lot of wrong reasons, and I'm sorry. But I still do want to be a part of the play. I want the play to be good, and please let me have the fun of helping that to happen.

"I know, Lord, you'll make it turn out right for all of us. Make Mrs. Clark's husband well, and help us to make this the best play that Westside playground has ever had. Give us all a happy ending. Amen."

Late that afternoon when the screen door slammed and Erica bounced into the kitchen, her mother nodded knowingly at her brother Paul.

"Guess what" Erica said.

"You got the Cinderella part," Mom guessed.

"Nope," Erica answered, but her face was glowing.

"You're going to be the ugliest stepsister," offered Paul.

Erica shot him a look of disgust. "No. Better. It's something that's happening for the first time in history."

"For the first time in history a girl will play the part of Prince Charming," her brother said.

"Quit that, Paul." There was a dramatic pause. "I'm going to be a student director," she said, lifting her chin in the air.

"Student director?"

"Yes. Remember how Mrs. Clark's husband was sick and we wondered if the play would have to be cancelled? Well, today before tryouts she talked to me about it, how she needed somebody to take charge each day until she gets there. She said she needed a dependable person, somebody who really cares about the play."

"And she picked you?" Mother asked.

"That's right. It's an important job, Mom, but Mrs. Clark thinks I can do it."

"And I think Mrs. Clark is right. I also think this calls for a celebration," Mom said, taking out the ice cream and the syrup for chocolate sundaes. "Oh, honey, I'm so proud of you. You must have prayed quite a prayer."

"Well, I did find out one thing, that God is there

—or better yet, that he's right here, and he really is listening."

Likewise the Spirit helps us in our weakness; for we do not know how to pray as we ought, but the Spirit himself intercedes for us.

Romans 8:26

I rattle off prayers, God, but I don't always think about what I'm saying. I guess I wouldn't blame you if you didn't even listen. But you do listen, Lord. I know sometimes you wait to answer, and sometimes the answer is no, but help me to understand your reasons. Amen

On Not Giving Up

My parents and my teachers get mad at me some-times because I don't finish things. I throw my proj-ects away or I stash them in my dresser drawer. Why can't everybody understand that it's because they're just not good enough?

"One more layer of sticks should do it," Ellen said to herself, carefully leaning them against each other in a sort of tepee arrangement. Then she scratched a match against the rough rock and stuck it between the twigs into a pile of brown pine needles. There was a little flare of flame, but it quickly faded into a thin curl of gray smoke, then died altogether. She struck another match, and then another, but each time the fire just smoldered briefly and died.

"I can't do it right. I can't even build a fire right," she said to herself.

A quick kick with her hiking shoe leveled the framework of sticks and wood chunks, and Ellen headed down the path to the lake without even looking back at the ruins of her fire. She sat awhile in the warm sand braiding three strands of grass together, then began smoothing the sand around her into a series of rounded hills. Dad found her there a little later.

"Want to take the canoe out for awhile, Ellen?" he asked.

Without comment she clambered into the stern of the canoe. As her father settled himself in the bow, she dug the handle of the paddle into the sandy lake bottom and helped to shove the canoe away from the shore.

It was peaceful on the lake. Turtles sunned themselves on rocks, then slipped off into the water, seeming to sense that something was coming too close. When a breeze rippled the surface, tall, furry weeds seemed to wriggle upwards through the water. Ellen scooped up a tadpole and watched it swim around for awhile in a puddle in her hand, then returned it to the water.

"Have a little trouble with your fire, Ellen?" Dad was trying to sound casual.

Ellen pulled the paddle through the water with several strong strokes, ignoring his question. Finally she said, "Oh, Daddy, you would have to find out. I guess I should have picked it apart instead of just kicking it down." Then she added, 'I did have a respectable woodpile. You always told us the secret of a good fire is to build a respectable woodpile."

Dad smiled. "Well, there's a little bit more to it

than just getting good wood. I think we can get that fire to work, but that isn't what worries me."

"What is?"

"To tell the truth, Ellen, I'm a little worried at the way you give up on yourself."

"I do?"

"That's right, and it's getting to be a habit, Ellen."

"What do you mean, a habit?"

"What ever happened to the tooled leather wallet you were making Grandpa for his birthday?"

"That's in my dresser drawer. I didn't get it done in time, so I bought him a scarf instead."

"And is that where you're keeping your half-finished latch hook pillow? You seemed so excited about joining 4-H, but you've dropped one project after another."

"Well, I keep changing my mind. I just find other projects I might like better."

"Is that the real reason, Ellen?"

"I guess not," she answered. "The real reason is that I'm not good at anything. I start out thinking I can do just about anything, but something always gets goofed up. I can tell it's not going to be any good, so I might just as well forget it. It hurts to admit it, Dad, but I can't do anything right."

Dad pulled his paddle out of the water and let the canoe drift for a minute. "Remember that little bird we were watching at the campsite this morning, Ellen?"

"The one trying to fly with a whole crust of bread?"

"That's the one. His flight was pretty wobbly, wasn't it? He might have decided to just drop the whole thing, but he didn't do that. He decided to

31

settle for a manageable crumb. That bird was being sensible. He scaled his load down to something he could handle."

"I guess I always thought it was good to want things to be just right," Ellen explained. "What's so bad about aiming high?"

"Remember that fishing trip to Lake Annabelle, Ellen? Remember how we kept throwing back every fish we caught, even some that were fairly big ones?"

"I remember, Dad. You kept saying, 'Well, that one's pretty small. We'd better throw it back.'"

"So you see, I do it too, Ellen. We all do. It's good to aim for the best, but at some point we have to look at what we do and then say to ourselves, 'Well, it's not perfect, but it could be worse. Looks to me like a keeper.' If we had done that at Lake Annabelle, at least we would have had a little taste of fish for dinner."

"Maybe if we really followed every rule for doing things, they would always turn out right."

"Well-l-l-, maybe. But I wonder, Ellen. You can learn all the rules about table manners. You can tell yourself a hundred times to keep your elbows off the table and your napkin in your lap, but when you're out some place eating, and the lettuce is falling out of your tuna fish sandwich or your water glass tips over, every rule you ever learned goes out the window."

"I guess the first Bible verse that Mrs. Swanson ever taught me in Sunday school was 'Be ye perfect.' Do you suppose God didn't mean it?"

Ellen's dad laughed at that.

"When God says 'Be ye perfect,' I don't think it's a demand for instant perfection. Becoming perfect

32

is a learning process, and God is nudging us to keep on with the process. He wants us to hang in there and keep moving toward what we're supposed to become."

"You mean he says, 'Be perfect, but it's OK if it doesn't happen this minute'?"

"Mm-hummm. And it doesn't even have to happen this day. Every kind of learning takes awhile, but becoming the new person God wants you to be takes a long while. It won't be finished, even when we come to the end of this little life."

"Dad, you told me awhile ago that I have the habit of giving up on myself. Now are you telling me that God won't give up on me?"

"You've got it. We can be useful long before we become perfect. God doesn't need to wait for our perfection before he can use us for his purposes. Keep your eyes open, and you'll find out that God has assignments for you to do. But God won't give up on you until the whole job is done. Unless you push him away, he's going to stick at the job of making you perfect."

A few minutes later Ellen's father pulled the canoe up on shore, then steadied it as Ellen cautiously made her way up the center of the canoe and stepped out on the wet sand.

"There's some unfinished business back at the campsite," he reminded her.

"Unfinished business? Oh, that," she said, shaking her head.

As they crouched in the ashes rebuilding the fire that Ellen had started earlier, her dad pointed out, "Your woodpile was respectable, all right—maybe even outstanding. But these pine needles were wet.

Let's try some of these dry leaves instead. It's important to have dry tinder."

"Is that why you're throwing out some of the little twigs? Are they wet, too?"

"No, Ellen, you've just crowded too much in there. There's got to be a good chimney for the air to flow through."

As Ellen scratched the match on the rock and touched it gently to the dry leaves, her dad heard her whisper to the flame, "Be ye perfect." Then she added in a louder voice. "But if you're not perfect, I've got lots of matches. This time I'm not giving up."

> Not that I have already obtained this or am already perfect; but I press on to make it my own, because Christ Jesus has made me his own.
>
> Philippians 3:12

I give up too easily, Lord. Just because something isn't good enough I quit trying. I know I'm far from perfect myself. That takes practice. But thank you for not giving up on me. Amen

My Friend Moved Away

My best friend moved away, and I feel so sad I can't stand it. Now who'll go with me on picnics and call me on the phone? Life will never be the same again.

"But she promised," Joanna said to herself. "Mary did make a promise that day of the auction. I guess she just didn't mean it."

Joanna sat in the tire swing. Her face was turned in the direction of the blacktop county road and the mailbox, but there was almost no expression on it. She wasn't really swinging, just walking the swing along with her feet, once in awhile pushing off, but mostly just thinking and remembering sadly the day of the auction sale at Gilman's farm.

In most ways the auction had been just like any auction. There was a grassy, makeshift parking lot across the road from Gilmans, with Mary's big brother, Scott, in charge of the parking. There were two hayracks cluttered with thick, rusty chains, drinking cups for hogs, weed cutters, cream cans, a typewriter, an old oak rocking chair.

Men dressed in jeans, dusty work boots, and mesh caps from the seed company stood around the racks talking to each other, listening to the sing-song chant of Walt Peterson, the auctioneer. Their faces were sober, and you could tell they didn't really believe it when he bragged about an old tractor that was parked by the barn.

But the auctioneer tried to joke them into a sale. "You'd look good in this one, Amos," he said, and Amos Hardy had to smile a little. Amos was too smart a farmer to get stuck with that old tractor, but he did smile.

On a folding table near the house were piles of plastic dishes, a box of green apples, canning jars, eggbeaters, a big gray crock. Women stood around the coffee maker, talking about the next Homemaker's meeting. Kids were grabbing handfuls of cookies from a plate, looking over the piles of old toys, and teasing the sleepy white cat who lay curled up under a lawn chair.

Yes, Joanna had been to a lot of auctions, and this one was like all the others, except for one thing. This time it was Mary who was moving away, and that hurt. It wasn't just that they enjoyed doing the same things, things like playing Aggravation or riding horses or rearranging furniture in Joanna's playhouse. It was the way she felt about Mary herself.

Mary could be really funny, but still she wasn't always showing off. When she told you she'd do

38

something, you could depend on her, and if you asked her to keep a secret, she'd keep it. Mary was the best friend she'd ever have. Joanna had signed her yearbook in three different places, just to make sure she'd remember.

Joanna picked up things from the folding table one at a time, looking at each item carefully. She had brought a little money along to bid on one thing, something that would always remind her of Mary.

Finally she found what she was looking for, a small white pitcher with a ring of blue flowers around its middle. That pitcher would remind her of all the nights she had stayed over at the Gilmans'. She'd remember whispering and giggling until past midnight and then getting up in the morning and having pancakes for breakfast, helping herself to syrup from that blue and white pitcher. When Mr. Peterson held it up and started his funny chanting, she hesitated a second, not exactly sure of how to do it, and Justin Garner's mother called out, "I'll bid 50 cents."

Joanna's hand felt sweaty and she clutched the three quarters in her sweater pocket. Her throat tightened up as she hollered, "Seventy-five!"

"Seventy-five, seventy-five." Mr. Peterson's eyes were raking over the crowd, looking for a higher bid. Justin's mother would bid higher, and Joanna knew that she didn't have enough money to keep on bidding. Then a good thing happened. Justin's mother just smiled at Joanna, and she didn't say another word, and neither did anybody else. The bidding had stopped.

So Joanna had carried the syrup pitcher home with her. She had also carried home Mary's promise to write a letter as soon as she got to her new home in Brockton.

That day had been hard, saying good-bye and everything, but not nearly so hard as waiting for Mary's letter. She tried to put it out of her mind, but Mary's promise kept playing tag with her thoughts.

Every day when she saw Russ Sorem's green station wagon coming along the blacktop road, she would take off for the mailbox at a dead run, with her dog Jesse trotting at her heels. Russ was their mailman. With his round bulb of a nose, his lumpy body, his old hat, and a pipe between his teeth, he reminded her a little of a melting snowman, but Joanna liked him. He seemed to care whether or not she got mail, and he always had time to talk. Joanna's mother said she bet he didn't make it home until midnight, if he visited that long at every mailbox.

Every day she and Jesse ran to the mailbox, and every day they brought back only things like seed catalogs and government pamphlets and her mother's Homemaker magazine. Russ tried to cheer her up about Mary.

"I wouldn't get too impatient with Mary, Joanna," he would say. "When you think about it, Mary had to leave a whole lot behind when she moved out of that big brick house. That isn't easy."

"Well, I guess not, Russ, but she's had almost two weeks to write."

"Two weeks seems like a long time when you're waiting," he said, "but not so long when you're working at getting settled. Try putting yourself in Mary's place, leaving everything she knew best. Here she knew every face on the school bus. She could think about which teacher she'd like for sixth grade because she already knew them."

"I know, and Brockton won't be like that, at least not for awhile. But, Russ, she promised."

Today would be different, Joanna decided. She wouldn't get her hopes up. The green station wagon was coming up the road, but that didn't mean she had to go running. She walked the swing to a stop, then reached down and picked up a little stick from the ground and threw it in the direction of the house.

"Go after it, Jesse," she said, but Jesse didn't listen. He was barking and tugging at the leg of her jeans with his teeth.

"Oh, all right," she said. "We'll go down there, but just to see Russ and pick up Mom's mail. Maybe Mary's forgotten all about me, but you're still my friend."

"How's it going, Joanna?" Russ Sorem asked, smiling through the open car window.

"I dunno, Russ. Nothing to do. Nobody to do it with."

"Still missing Mary Gilman, right, Joanna?"

"You're right. But I'm not counting on a letter. It's been four weeks, so I guess she just won't be keeping her promise."

"Well, as I said, Joanna, I'll bet moving so far away has been really scary for her. If you're her friend, you should be almost glad that she's so busy doing things that there's no time for letters. If all of Mary's fun is what fits into a mailbox, she'll be spending a lot of lonely hours. You wouldn't want that for her."

"But what do I do for a friend?" She dug her fingers into the fur around her dog's ears. "Jesse is my

friend, but I can't spend all day just throwing sticks for Jesse to chase."

"Well, how about Valerie, that red-haired girl who just moved into the Siewert home place? Seems like a nice girl."

"Her?"

"Well, why not?"

"Well, for one thing, nobody wears her hair in a pony tail any more, and she comes to school all the time in a dress, just like she was going to have her picture taken, and, well, she's always doing or saying something weird, just to get attention. She keeps telling everybody she's got a horse. They know it by now, but she keeps bringing it up. Kind of bragging."

"You mean she's trying too hard?"

"That's it. She's trying too hard. She laughs when nothing is funny, and she acts bold and pushy. Sometimes I feel sort of sorry for her, but Mary always said that—" Joanna stopped speaking. It might be better not to tell Russ Sorem what Mary had said.

"The way I see it, Joanna, this isn't Mary's problem. This is between you and Valerie. The hard thing about friendship is that the people who need friends the most—girls like Valerie, for example— are the people who have the least skill at making friends."

"That's Valerie," Joanna agreed.

"Valerie probably started off with a handicap because her mother keeps her in that out-of-date hair style, and Valerie feels so different and left out that she can't just act natural. She keeps trying too hard. I'll bet that if she knew she had one friend she'd be

43

able to relax and be herself and then everyone would like her better."

"You seem to know a lot about girls, Russ. It's hard to believe you've never been one."

"No," Russ smiled, "but I've raised four of 'em. Not too many brand-new problems come along. I do know that Mary can't choose your friends for you by remote control. You've got to feel free to choose your own."

"Maybe Mary has decided it's too hard to be friends with somebody who lives 116 miles away," Joanna said.

"You'll always be her friend, Joanna, but maybe she can't be your everyday friend any more. Why can't she be your fifth grade friend?"

"Yes, I suppose she can still be my vacation friend, or my friend in Brockton."

"Do you have a doll that you loved when you were little, I mean more than all the rest?"

"Of course. She had blonde hair and freckles, and I named her Anne Marie."

"Still play with that doll, Joanna?"

"Well, not really. Some days I hardly remember I have her, but every once in awhile I take her out and play with her for a little bit, and I do still love her."

"People just don't stay put these days, you know. I see how people keep changing their addresses, even farm people, and there's a whole lot of saying good-bye. Trying to hang on too hard is like clutching a butterfly. You'll just wreck your friendship the minute you try to do that."

"You mean it's so beautiful that you want it to stay, but if you crush it, it's no longer beautiful?"

"That's true, Joanna. I guess the best way is to keep adding to your collection of friends, and that way there's always somebody around when you want to go biking or skating."

"I guess so. Maybe Valerie could ride her bike over here this afternoon. Guess I'll call her." She turned to go, then remembered something. "Say, Russ, do you have any mail for my mom or dad?"

"'Fraid not, Joanna, but there is a letter here addressed to you."

"A letter? For me?" The address up in the corner read "Brockton." "Oh, Russ, I thought you were my friend. How come you kept me worried?"

By this time she had torn a ragged strip from the end of the envelope and was reading Mary's words:

"I've met some kids at school, and one of them asked me to go swimming at the pool in town. They're kind of friendly and they seem nice. I'm hoping I'll get used to it here, but I can hardly wait 'til vacation."

Joanna nodded. Mary would be her vacation friend. Then she read the last paragraph: "Don't forget, Joanna. First I'm going back there for a week, and then I want you to spend a week here. OK?"

"OK," Joanna said out loud. She stuffed the letter back into the envelope and started running toward the house, with Jesse barking at her heels.

There are friends who pretend to be friends, but there is a friend who sticks closer than a brother.

Proverbs 18:24

45

My friend moved away, Lord, but friendship didn't. We can find ways to keep in touch, and we can both have fun with new friends. Stay by me today, God, and show me how to be a good friend. Amen

Why the Big Secret?

The T-shirt seemed like a neat thing to buy when I was at church camp. Everybody up there was wearing one. But I don't really like to wear it back home. How come Mother keeps asking about that shirt? It's no big deal.

"Is my green T-shirt in the dryer, Mom? I'm going outside for awhile."

"It's not dry yet, Kristi. Why not wear that one you bought up at camp?"

Kristi breathed a big sigh. "I don't like the way it fits. It's the green one I want."

"It really looks just fine on you, Kristi. What's the problem with that shirt? You seemed to like the fit well enough when we were up there for Parents' Day, and I've been really careful not to shrink it in the wash."

"Let's just skip it, Mom, OK?" Kristi snapped. "I'll wait for the green one."

"Kristi, are you sure you—never mind. Maybe I shouldn't have said anything."

Kristi jammed her fists into the pockets of her robe and stomped down the stairs to the laundry room. Her eyes fastened on the window in the dryer as if it were a TV screen. As the colored clothes tumbled past her view, once in awhile she caught a glimpse of the green shirt. "The clothes are really tossing around now. Must be almost ready," she thought.

Why did Mother keep bugging her about that T-shirt? Maybe she wasn't getting enough wear out of it, but it was no big deal. At camp she had really wanted that shirt. Everybody else was wearing one, and it seemed important. Up there it had been fun to sing songs about God at the dinner table, it had been fun around the campfire sharing feelings with each other, even fun sitting under the trees studying the Bible. Wearing the camp T-shirt was a way of saying, "I like it here."

But back in town she felt kind of funny running around in a shirt that said "Camp of the Living Word." How could she explain about it to the other kids whose shirts pictured Yellowstone National Park or Disneyworld or Snoopy? Everybody knew without asking what their shirts were about.

When the tumbling clothes had slowed down, then settled at the bottom of the dryer, Kristi opened the door and pulled out the warm green shirt, with its white-lettered message: "My Room Off Limits— Disaster Area."

A few minutes later as she walked her bike out of the garage, Kristi noticed Jessica Morton washing

"Different? In what way, Kristi?"

"Well, up there I was really proud of that shirt. The camp was like a special little world. It seemed like everything we talked about or thought about that week was clean and good. Even when we admitted our sins or talked about problems, we felt safe, like there was a good answer to everything. And when we all wore those shirts, it was like saying we all agreed about the answer. We all stood for the same thing. Jesus really was the Living Word."

"And now that you're home? Didn't you bring your faith home with you, Kristi?"

"Well, I still believe that stuff we learned, Jessica, but—"

"But back here, you're not sure everybody else does?"

"That's about it. I almost feel odd when I wear it. I just feel like keeping quiet about camp—not running it down or anything, just keeping quiet."

"Maybe you're almost ashamed of it?"

Kristi nodded. "That's right. Almost ashamed."

Jessica laid down her soapy sponge and brushed her hair back with her forearm before picking up the hose again. Her face grew sober. "It's funny, Kristi. I think I felt the same way after one year at camp. It's easy to wear a sort of badge of Christianity at camp where everybody does it. It's the thing to do, and nobody challenges you there. But back home, if you're different, it's noticed. We shrink from that. We all do."

"I figured I was the only one who felt that way," Kristi said.

"When God created us, Kristi, he didn't cut us

Our New Baby Can't Hear

They say my new baby sister is deaf, that she'll never hear anything in her whole life. Does that mean she can never be happy?

"You're Amanda, aren't you?"

The last tinkly notes of "Away in a Manger" came to a sudden stop as Amanda snapped the cover shut on the manger scene and slipped the music box into the plastic shopping bag.

Amanda hadn't seen the tall, smiling lady cross the lobby and approach the green sofa where she sat alone.

"Yes, I'm Amanda," she nodded, "but—"

"I'm Jeanne Seaton, the patient's representative for this wing of the hospital. It's my job to help patients with problems that come up. Your mother heard you were down here and that you have a pres-

what would it be like to be in a world where you couldn't understand what anybody was saying?"

Amanda tried to imagine it.

"Well, we were in Mexico once, and I didn't understand a word. I really felt left out. Or maybe being deaf would be like watching TV when the sound isn't working. It would be awful."

"You're right, Amanda. It isn't easy. It wouldn't be easy to be in a room full of people and, as you sat there waiting for something to make sense, suddenly everyone laughed and you didn't even know what the joke was about."

"I guess there would be other things. Like how could you know when there was a knock on the door or when a policeman blows his whistle?"

"That's right. Or when the loudspeaker at the pizza place announces that your order is ready. Those are some of the things that Erin will have to deal with."

Amanda nodded. "Now maybe you know why I just don't want to go up there. It might not be right, but I just can't do it."

"I do understand, Amanda. Well, OK. Let's forget about that for awhile. Right now there's a place I'd like you to go with me. It's not far from here. We can walk."

"I don't know. I did promise Dad I'd stay right here."

"Tell you what. Why don't I call your Mom's room and check it out with your Dad. OK? This is important, Amanda."

Miss Seaton slipped into the phone booth near the reception desk and made the call. Amanda could see her smiling, then nodding, then smiling again.

Whatever Jeanne Seaton's plan was, it must be OK with Dad.

"Better take the present with you," Miss Seaton said. Amanda picked up the bag and walked with her out through the big front doors and down Hancock Street, wondering where they were going and why. She was even more puzzled a few minutes later as they turned up the brick sidewalk to what looked like a small church. The gold-lettered sign by the door told her she was right. "Church of the Master's Touch" it read. To church? On a Thursday afternoon?

Inside the door, in the entry, Amanda noticed a huge red and yellow banner with the words "Praise the Lord" across the top. She had seen banners with those words on them before, but never one like this. Covering the whole banner were pictures of hands, hands with fingers pointing in every possible direction. And on every hand was somebody's signature.

"Miss Seaton—"

"Why don't you call me Jeanne?"

"Jeanne, why do you suppose—?"

"Let's talk about it later, Amanda. We don't want to miss the choir practice."

"Choir practice? I don't hear any singing. It sounds like a piano playing somewhere, but nobody is singing."

A few seconds later, when they went into the big room at the end of the hall, Amanda began to see why.

There were kids in the room, all right, kids of a lot of different sizes. They weren't singing, but they seemed to be moving their hands in time with the music, almost like dancers sometimes do, all making

"OK. Does everybody you know think of you as the girl who doesn't know how to whistle?"

"I guess not. I hope not. I can't whistle, but there are lots of things I can do."

"Well, your baby sister is the same way. She can't hear. She'll never be able to hear, but her deafness isn't the only thing about her. Maybe it isn't even the most important thing about her."

Amanda looked through the nursery window at all the boxlike little beds, straining her eyes to read the names on the pink bracelets because those were for the girls. She looked at the bed closest to her. That baby was red and wrinkly with a head that came to a point, and she was screaming her head off. Could that be her sister? No, the tag read "Winston Girl."

Now the nurse was wheeling another bed right up to the window and smiling at Amanda through the glass. Could this be her sister? This baby was a lovely, pale shade of pink, with a fuzzy cap of brown hair. She almost seemed to be smiling at her fist, and the tag said "Erin."

"Now," Jeanne said, "tell me what you see."

"Well, her eyes are blue."

"Good. They may turn brown a little later, but right now they are blue. And what else?"

"Well, she looks just perfect, even—"

"Even her ears?"

"Even her ears." Amanda breathed more easily now. She added, "I think she looks happier than the others."

"You know, I think you're right. Remember what we said about her deafness not being the most important thing about her? Who knows? Maybe she'll be good at art, or she could be a great basketball

Then the eyes of the blind shall be opened, and the ears of the deaf unstopped.

Isaiah 35:5

I feel sad sometimes, Lord, because some people are born with terrible problems, like not being able to hear. They have to learn new ways to do things. Show me new ways to help them, God. And thank you for all the other things they can do. Amen

The Gigglers and God

The other kids in my Sunday school class act terrible in church. They get the giggles and they mess around with the bulletins. They're really not all that nice, so how come it bothers me when they go off and do things without me?

"Wait a second, and I'll go with you," Katie said, but the others didn't seem to hear her. They were already halfway out of the door of the church school classroom, laughing as they walked into the hall and headed toward the pop machine.

Katie looked stricken, but recovered quickly and turned toward her teacher. "OK if I help you wash off the tables, Mrs. Owens? And I'll put the modeling clay into the plastic bags."

"Well, fine," Mrs. Owens said, "but if you're looking for a job, I'd really like help in hanging this stained-glass mural. It's so long I can't manage."

Katie picked up one end of the long strip of paper colored to look like a stained-glass window and held it up to the wall. "Is this about right?"

"Fine, but Katie, are you sure you don't want to catch up with the others?"

"No, it's OK." Katie's voice clipped off each word. "I think I'd really rather sit alone at the services."

"You're sure?"

"I'm sure. It seems like I'm the only one in the whole class that knows how you're supposed to behave in church." Katie's tone grew confidential. "You should just see how they act, Mrs. Owens. Sometimes when they're waiting for worship to start they play this little game of staring each other down. And they always end up getting the giggles. They don't even know what being reverent means."

"What does it mean, Katie?"

The question surprised Katie. "Well, doesn't it mean being quiet and respectful in church? It certainly doesn't mean talking and laughing and fooling around."

"I guess I have a little different idea about that, Katie. There's a verse in the Bible about being glad when someone invites us to go unto the house of the Lord. To me, *glad* is really the key word."

"Is it wrong to try to be quiet in church?"

"Well, what God wants most is a world full of happy, loving people. He doesn't demand that we all walk on tiptoe and speak in whispers. You love God, don't you, Katie, and you want to do whatever it takes to please him, right?"

"I really do. Being quiet in church just feels right to me."

"And that's neat. I'm sure God is your friend. But it's important to remember that he has other friends too, friends who don't always stay quiet in church. I believe God loves kids even when they're giggling."

Katie squeezed a piece of modeling clay between her fingers for a minute before dropping it into the bag. "I hadn't thought about it, but Jesus didn't really leave a lot of instructions about behaving yourself in church, did he? I guess that's because he didn't come to be a rule-maker. You've always told us he came to show us what love means."

"No, he didn't spend a lot of time talking about church behavior," her teacher agreed, "but do you remember that one story about a church leader and a tax collector going to church to pray?"

"I remember. The tax collector was a well-known sinner. I think the point of Jesus' story was that the sinner prayed a better prayer than the church leader did."

"Right. Do you know what self-righteousness means?"

"I'm not sure," Katie said, "but I guess it's like the church leader in the story. The church leader built up his own picture of himself by comparing himself with the tax collector. He even thanked God that he was better than the other guy."

"You've got it, Katie. It is important that everyone learns sometime to come quietly to God. You happened to learn it sooner than the others, but meanwhile there are worse things than getting the giggles in church."

"I guess the worst thing would be to sit in church and think you're better than everybody else."

'Sure. God wants honesty from us."

"Honesty?"

"Yes. We should just be ourselves. We should go into church as sinners who see their own sinfulness. If we weren't sinners we wouldn't even need a Savior."

There was a troubled expression in Katie's eyes. "Lately I've felt like I don't have any friends at church, Mrs. Owens."

"I'm sure the girls don't snub you because of your goodness, Katie, but maybe there's something about your goodness that's hard to take. Maybe they just don't have as much fun when you're around. It's hard work to be friends with somebody who's scolding you all the time."

"I guess that's true," Katie said. "When I was little, there was this lady at the public library whose full-time job was shushing people. I got so I didn't even like to read books."

Her teacher laughed at that. "Exactly! Why don't you give your friends a little time, Katie? They'll learn gradually to behave themselves in church. As they grow up, the giggling will quiet down. They'll come to understand that their giggling can spoil it for the other people who are trying to concentrate on prayer. But I hope they don't ever grow out of the idea that church is a nice place to be. It's meant to be a place of love and warmth and friendliness. God wants us all to be happy here."

And Jesus answered them, "Those who are well have no

need of a physician, but those who are sick; I have not come to call the righteous, but sinners to repentance."

Luke 5:31-32

You're not a rule-maker, Jesus, so how come I try to make rules for everybody else? What makes me think I'm so much better than the other kids? Put me to work on my own faults, so I won't have time to notice everybody else's. And, Jesus, help me to see your smile. Amen

Teamwork Pays Off

There's this one kid I know who always has to do everything I do. Why can't he think up his own stuff? How come it bugs me most when he does the same thing and beats me at it?

Bridget made a fist and punched it into the hollow of the catcher's mitt. She twisted the mitt back and forth, looked once more at Johnny Bench's name scrawled on the leather, and slowly laid it back on the counter.

Some of those boys still thought that girls shouldn't be on the team. How could she change their minds if she didn't even have a mitt? Bridget dug down into her jeans pocket for her blue plastic coin purse and squeezed it open. Still only four dimes and one nickel—same as five minutes ago. She walked out through the checkout, empty-handed.

There had to be a way. Allowance day was Tuesday, but it would take her birthday money and all of her allowances for six weeks to pay for that mitt.

Chris Duncan had had a toy sale last week, and she made $3.78, but that was different. Chris Duncan had lots of books that nobody had read. Chris Duncan's Barbie Doll had dresses she hadn't even worn. No wonder she made money. Bridget's own battered pile of cast-off toys was clearly not in the same class.

How about a Kool-Aid stand? Mother had said just last week, "No more Kool-Aid stands until you're through college," but that was the day the washing machine broke down. It hadn't been a good day for Mother. She had seemed cheerful enough this morning. Well, it was worth a try.

"Mom, if I promise to use no more than two flavors, and if I fill the ice cube trays when I'm done, and if I don't make Mrs. Engberg buy eight cupfuls, can I please have a Kool-Aid stand today?"

Bridget had guessed right. Her mother was in a good mood and gave her reluctant approval to a one-day stand.

Bridget set to work tearing open the envelopes, running the cold water, tugging the big spoon through the mountain of sugar at the bottom of each pitcher. Then she lugged a patio bench out to the curb and lined up the paper cups on it. When the cold pitchers and the muffin pan were in place, she leaned her cardboard sign against a tree: "Fresh Kool-Aid—5 Cents."

She had been too busy to notice the activity across the street at Cooper's house, but now she glanced up and discovered the truth. Danny Cooper was setting

up a Kool-Aid stand of his own! Not even one nickel in her muffin pan yet, and Danny was in business! It happened every time. Whenever Bridget did something, Danny had to do the same thing. And he usually beat her at it.

Billy and Joshua came pumping up the street on their tricycles. As they passed Bridget's stand they slowed down, looked soberly at the Kool-Aid pitchers, and climbed off their trikes.

"S'pose we could have some Kool-Aid?" asked Billy.

"Got a nickel?"

"No," Josh answered, "we don't have any money, but we're thirsty." Then, hesitantly, "We've got a rock—"

"Well," Bridget said weakly, "I guess you can each have a half a cup. But don't tell any other kids you got it free."

Her little customers looked happy, but the muffin cups were still empty.

Well, if Bridget's business was slow, so was Danny's. Kids passed by on the street, sometimes stopping to talk, but—well, maybe it was too soon after breakfast.

Bridget stacked and unstacked paper cups while she was waiting. It gave her something to do. She looked over at Danny straightening out his sign. Why didn't he just give up?

Now the ice cubes were melting. Why not set the pitchers over in the shade, just until business picked up? She noticed Danny was gone for a minute, then came back and held up an ice cube tray, tumbling the cubes into his big pail.

A gust of wind swept down the street, knocking over a stack of paper cups on Danny's table. Bridget looked away so she wouldn't smile and managed to whistle instead.

Bridget's mother came out with a nickel. "I'm thirsty, honey, could I have a cup of the orange?"

Well, Mother was nice, but Bridget didn't really see this as any big new hope.

"Mom, could I have a sandwich?"

"Sure, I'll bring one out."

"And how about some more ice cubes? They're down to little slivers now."

Maybe noontime would be better. Kool-Aid could be like dessert for the kids in the neighborhood.

She looked at her sign. Could that be the trouble? She took out an orange crayon and changed it to read, "Best Fresh Kool-Aid in Town—5 Cents."

Soon that brought a change in Danny's sign: "Best Kool-Aid in the World—4 Cents."

Four cents! Wow! Now her price would have to go down.

Bridget decided, "Before I run out of crayons and cardboard, I'd better talk to Danny."

"Danny," she hollered, "come over here a minute."

"Can't," Danny shook his head. "I can't leave my stand during business hours."

Bridget put her hands on her hips and looked down at the ground a minute. Then she scooped Mother's nickel out of the muffin cup and stuffed it in her shirt pocket, flicked a brown bug off the lip of the Kool-Aid pitcher, glanced up and down the streets for cars, then ran over to Danny's stand.

"Business isn't so good for you either, huh?"

"Nope," Danny admitted.

"I'd sure like to get some money for that mitt," Bridget said.

"Yeah, and I got a chance to go to the circus if I can save up two dollars."

"What do you suppose we should do?"

"I don't know," Danny said. "I think when the ice melts this time, I'll give up."

Bridget was more stubborn than that. "Danny, when do people drink Kool-Aid?"

"When they're thirsty."

"I guess you're right. They don't buy it because I need a new catcher's mitt or because you want to go to the circus. No, they buy it because they're thirsty."

Danny had a thought. "We have to find thirsty customers. But how?"

Bridget got a little excited. "I get most thirsty from running hard or from eating crackers."

Danny frowned. "Ohhh, right. How do we find kids who've been running hard or eating crackers?"

Bridget shook her head. "We don't, Danny. We don't *find* them thirsty. We *make* them thirsty."

They made their plans. There was still a half day left, and the weather *was* getting warmer. First they took their last pieces of cardboard and made two big signs that read: "Willow Street Summer Games —Beginning Very Soon—Games Free—Small Charge for Refreshments—Ask Me."

Then they tied the boards together with strings and hung them over Danny so one covered his front and one covered his back.

"OK, Bridget. I'll go around the neighborhood and

get the kids. You move your Kool-Aid things to my table and get ready for when the kids start to come."

Danny walked off down the street, leaving Bridget to tend the store. She called to her mother to ask for a basket of crackers. Then she made two small signs, one reading "Races Here" and the other, "Cracker-Eating Contest." Then she waited for Danny's return.

When Danny came back, he had two girls with him, Lucy and Kathy Engel from over on Elm Street.

"There'll be more coming," Danny assured her. "Let's get set up. I'll run the races over in your yard, and you can stay here and do the cracker-eating contest. Think you can do that and sell Kool-Aid?"

"I think so," Bridget said, with growing confidence.

Neighborhood kids began to come—one or two at a time at first, then more—mostly to see what was going on. But soon curiosity turned into excitement, and the prospect of free crackers lured them to enter the wild competition, stuffing them into their mouths, the crushed pieces falling down their chins. Danny's mother brought more crackers, and the Kool-Aid sales grew brisk.

Bridget smiled in triumph as she emptied the last of the Kool-Aid pitchers and looked at the piles of coins in the muffin tin. As she began sorting them into her stack and Danny's stack, she thought, "One more allowance day and I'll have that catcher's mitt."

"Danny," she grinned, "the business was here all the time. All we needed was an idea."

Danny nodded in agreement. "And we needed something else—teamwork. My dad always says, 'If you can't lick 'em, join 'em.' Right?"

79

Finally, all of you, have unity of spirit, sympathy, love of the brethren, a tender heart and a humble mind.

1 Peter 3:8

It's dumb, isn't it, Lord, worrying so much about beating somebody else? That way everybody loses. Teach me what teamwork means. Amen

Closeness and Distance

My mother always snoops around in my room. She opens my letters too. I don't have any really bad secrets, but they're mine. I get mad when Mom goes into my things without asking. Is that terrible?

Mother pulled the plug and wound the cord around the vacuum cleaner, then began to dust the things on Emily's desk.

"Why in the world does she keep that old thing?" she wondered, dusting under a bedraggled stuffed turtle.

Then she picked up the thick little book with the plaid cover. Linda Walters smiled to herself. "Emily certainly has been faithful about writing in this diary. Every day, as regular as a clock. It's fun to see her so interested, but I wonder what she finds to write about."

Casually, she opened the cover and began to read the entry dated June 27.

"Dear Diary," she read, "I'm mad. This time I'm really mad."

A little startled, she read cn: "It's Mother. Today I found her reading my letter from Trish. There were no big secrets in it—nothing I'd be ashamed to have her read or anything—but it was my letter. That's important to me. It was my letter. She should have asked. I suppose I'll forgive her sometime, but right now I'm mad."

The last line was underlined. Quickly Emily's mother shut the diary and set it down on the desk, feeling guilty and confused.

Later, when Emily got back from roller skating, her mother tried to talk with her:

"Emily, I realize now how you feel about Trish's letter."

"Mother, you didn't! You've been reading my diary, too."

"Yes, I read that one page, but—"

Emily stalked past her into her bedroom, slamming the door behind her. Her mother waited a few minutes, then tapped at the door.

"Emily, could we talk about it?"

"There's nothing to say."

"We do have an agreement about these things, Emily. We've promised each other to talk things out."

A long silence, then Emily slowly opened the door, her face rigid, like somebody getting ready to blow up a balloon.

"Emily, I've read your diary for the last time."

Emily answered her with a prickly silence.

"If you want my apology, you've got it," her mother said softly. Again, silence. "Maybe it wouldn't help you to talk about this, but it would certainly help me," Mother said, sitting down on the edge of the bed.

Emily's expression softened a little. She breathed a long sigh. "Mom, I really do want my things left alone."

"I know that. Now I know how important it is to you."

"Well, then, why did you—" She hesitated. "Why were you snooping?"

"That word smarts a little, but OK, I'll try to tell you why. I've been trying to understand it myself. You see, when you were little, I had to take charge of your whole life. Babies wouldn't survive without parents to watch over them almost every minute. Right?"

"OK, but I haven't been a baby for a long time. Please don't treat me like one."

"Even when you got a little bigger, it was still my job to sort through your clothes and toys and decide what should be thrown away. I've had to clean your dresser drawers and help you answer letters and check to see that your room is in shape."

"I can understand that," Emily admitted.

"I've managed to keep pretty good track of how many inches you've grown, but I didn't even notice that your feelings are growing up too. Maybe it's lucky I snooped today."

Emily stiffened. She glared at her mother.

"Oh, sure. Lucky."

"Well, if I hadn't, it might have taken awhile to

see that it's time to give you a little room for becoming a separate person."

"A separate person?"

"Yes, Emily. I've done a lot of thinking today about families. It seems to me that a family needs some closeness and some distance, a little of each. If we love each other, we should feel close. If we respect each other, we should grant each other some distance. There should be both time together and time to be alone. You're hurting for more privacy, right?"

"Right. A lot more."

"OK. I should have noticed you were old enough to have feelings about privacy. But maybe I should also have noticed you were old enough to clean your own room."

"By myself?"

"Why not? What was I doing in there dusting and vacuuming? And certainly you're quite capable of keeping your own drawers in order."

"Well, OK, Mom. I guess if you hadn't been dusting in here you wouldn't have looked in the diary. Maybe I could learn to do the cleaning."

"And you know, honey, privacy goes both ways."

"I'm not sure I understand that."

"Now that you've come to value your own privacy, can I count on you to respect mine?"

"Like how?"

"Well, you don't want me bursting into your room without knocking, but I have those same feelings. Maybe I'm dressing or trying to think through a problem. Sometimes your Dad and I just want to be alone."

"I guess I never thought about that."

"Another thing, Emily. You've felt free to rum-

mage around in my drawers looking for sticky tape
or a blow dryer or a scissors. I'm not too crazy about
finding my drawers all rearranged. No, that's too
polite a word. They're a disaster after you've gone
to work on them."

"But sometimes I need the tape, and you know,
Mom, there is only one decent scissors in this house."
Emily thought it over, frowning a little, then suddenly looked at her mother. "You know, Mom, I've
always complained about having so many rules, but
maybe we need just a few new ones, some rules
about privacy."

"Why not?" Mom agreed. "We could spell out
what rights each of us should have, rules that would
help us to keep both closeness and distance. You
should have the right to be alone in your room, even
to lock your door, and I should knock before I come
in."

"And I guess you and Daddy should have that
same right. And I'd like to be able to talk on the
phone without your standing at my elbow or picking up the extension," Emily said.

"That's another rule that should go both ways."

"And no reading of letters or diaries without per-
mission. OK, Mom?"

"You've got it."

"And if I clean my room, you'll stay away from my
drawers?"

"Yes, and you will do the same. Maybe things
that we all use, things like shampoo and tape and
scissors, could be kept in a neutral area. Some places
should be everybody's territory."

"Like the kitchen or the bathroom, or maybe the
den?"

86

"Yes, that should work out. If we keep the blow dryer in the bathroom and the sticky tape and writing paper and scissors in the desk, we've already solved some of our traffic problems."

"Sounds all right to me, Mom."

"Remember, Emily, we don't have the right to lock doors against each other's interest and love. I hope you'll never feel that your happiness is none of my business. And none of us has the right to lie or to be dishonest with each other."

"I'm not asking for that right, Mom. I want to be treated like a separate person, but I'm a separate person who likes being a part of this family."

Linda Walters gave her daughter a quick squeeze, then left the room, quietly shutting the door behind her.

> Be angry but do not sin; do not
> let the sun go down on your
> anger.
>
> Ephesians 4:26

We're a family, God, but we're separate persons too. We need to be together and we need to be alone. Help us to be patient with each other as we look for the right mix of closeness and distance. Amen

What If People Find Out?

I'm worried about my mother lately. I think she drinks more than she should. How can I keep everybody else from finding it out?

"Heather, I was looking for your mother to come for a conference yesterday. Do you happen to know why she wasn't able to make it?"

Heather's brown eyes were guarded, even fearful. She lifted her chin and looked straight across the desk at Mr. Chellberg. Words of explanation began to tumble out.

"Well, you see, Mother woke up with a bad cold, and my little brother is sick, and my Dad had asked her to take care of some business for him, and . . . and. . . ."

Heather's voice trailed off into a whisper, and she looked down at the floor. Mr. Chellberg nodded. "I think I understand, Heather. Shall I call her for another appointment?"

"Well, I suppose you could, but I'm not sure—" Heather gulped. "Maybe it's better if—"

Mr. Chellberg was startled to see that there were tears standing in Heather's eyes.

"I didn't mean to upset you, Heather. If your mother would rather not come, I understand. If there's anything you'd like to tell me about what the problem is, that's fine, but it's up to you."

There was a long pause. "Sometimes I wish I could, Mr. Chellberg. It's so hard, worrying about it all alone, but it's just too awful." She wiped tears away with the back of her hand.

"I may be way off the mark, Heather, and you don't have to answer this, but is there a problem with drinking?"

Heather looked startled, then asked weakly, "How did you know about that, Mr. Chellberg? I didn't think anybody knew. I didn't want anybody to know."

Her thoughts went back through all of the months since she began to learn the dreadful secret. She hadn't thought too much about it at first, but things began to change around the house.

Heather would come home from school and find her mother taking a nap. Sometimes she would be sleeping so hard that Heather would get worried and shake her awake. Her mother would get up and start doing things in the kitchen, but she moved too carefully, almost like a movie in slow motion.

Then there was a day off from school, the day of a teachers' meeting. She noticed that her mother sat down at the kitchen table as soon as Dad left for work that morning, and that she was drinking something brownish with ice cubes in it. By noon it seemed to her that Mom's voice was a little slurred, and there was an unpleasant smell on her breath.

The rest of that day was a kind of nightmare. Her little brother, Charlie, wandered out of the yard by himself, and Mom didn't even seem to notice. Then, after a long nap, her mother asked Heather to fix hamburgers so that dinner would be ready when Dad came home.

"How hot shall I set the stove?"

Mom looked at her dully, shook her head a little, then laughed for no reason, "Lesh shee—how hot shall we make it?"

Well, Mr. Chellberg had guessed the secret anyway, so maybe she should tell him. All at once she heard herself talking about the day of the teachers' meeting and about a lot of other things, things that she had thought she'd never tell anybody. She had held the secret in for so long that it felt good now to talk about it.

She told him about how her mother tried to hide her problem from the family. There was that time when Heather opened a vanilla bottle and smelled that same strong odor that she had noticed on Mother's breath. Afraid and ashamed, she had put it back on the shelf, half hoping that her dad wouldn't find out.

"You know, Mr. Chellberg, when I find one of Mom's bottles I want to pour that stuff right down the sink, so she can't drink it. Once I did it, but Mom caught me at it. I'll never forget how mad she got, and how hard she cried."

Mr. Chellberg shook his head. "You can pour

liquor down the sink, but that won't solve anything because you can't pour her need for it down the sink. Does your mother make excuses, does she think up elaborate reasons why she drinks?"

"Well, yes. One time she's had a bad day, or the world is in awful shape, or a neighbor has said something to hurt her feelings. Mr. Chellberg, I just hate it when she tries to force me to hug her. I can't stand the smell of the liquor, and it's just as bad when she tries to cover it up with mouthwash."

Most of all Heather hated it when she began to hear her parents quarreling. Usually they argued behind a closed door, but Heather heard the same phrases repeated again and again.

Her Mom would say, "Let's not start on that."

Then Dad would insist, "I do care about you, Anne—too much to let this happen to you. It would hurt you the worst if anything happened to Charlie."

When Mom did promise to taper off cn the drinking, her father sounded impatient. "I've heard that promise before."

Tuesday night was the worst. Mom was screaming, "I'm sick of being checked up on," and Dad answered, "You'd better get used to it."

Then she heard the talk about a separation and the crying at the end.

"You see, Mr. Chellberg, Mom isn't herself right now, but I love her anyway because I don't think she can help it."

"Do you and your father talk about this much?" Mr. Chellberg asked gently.

Heather shook her head. "It's like we pretend to each other that nothing is happening. We can't talk, and we can't work it out, and it seems like nothing can be done about it."

"Not true, Heather." Her teacher's voice was firm now. "I know it's not true."

"How can you know that?"

"Well, you've shared your secret with me, and so I'm going to share something with you. I'm an alcoholic. All those things you've told me about your mother's behavior are things that once happened to me. My wife and children were hurt by it just as much as you are now."

Mr. Chellberg—her favorite teacher? The teacher that every kid in school hoped they'd get for fifth grade?

"But you're—"

"You mean I don't act like your mother? That's because I'm sober now, Heather. I don't drink any more, but I'll always be an alcoholic. That means I can't handle liquor. I can never drink safely. If I started to drink at all, I'd be right back in that miserable trap."

"But how did you get over it? I don't think my mother could stop drinking now. It's like she's fighting some terrible battle and she can't figure out a way to win it. I guess we'd need a miracle to straighten things out."

"That's right, a healing miracle," he said. "You see, it's a kind of sickness, and the whole family becomes infected with it. Everybody lies. Everybody covers up. Everybody feels guilty. It's a sickness of the spirit that grabs a whole household. Everybody feels so ashamed of the problem that nobody dares to ask for help."

"But where do we find our miracle?"

"Well, the best thing that ever happened to me was Alcoholics Anonymous."

"Alcoholics Anonymous?"

"It's sort of like a club, Heather—a club for people who need help with their drinking and have reached the point where they admit they need it."

"I'm not sure my Mom would admit it. She doesn't admit it to my Dad."

"She has to start at the beginning. Somehow she has to learn to admit it to herself first and then to her family and finally to everybody. She has to learn from other alcoholics that being ashamed can't set things right. She needs a new recipe for hope."

"A new recipe?"

"Yes, it's a recipe we alcoholics have for keeping ourselves sober, and we call it the Twelve Steps. The first step—and the most important one—is learning to turn our troubles over to God. Without his help, it's just about impossible."

"I'm not sure she would ever turn over her troubles to God. Mom doesn't go to church lately."

"That doesn't mean she doesn't believe in God, or she doesn't love him. Right now she's feeling guilty —afraid. She doesn't trust God to help her with her problems."

"What are some of the other steps?"

"Well, things like learning to take on problems one at a time, or learning to make up for the hurt we've caused others. A really helpful step is learning to use the hotline, calling up other members when we feel a terrible need to take a drink."

"What can they do?"

"They can come running to help—and they do— even at three o'clock in the morning. When I called people, they didn't help me to cover up. They encouraged me to face my problem honestly. The last step in my own recovery, the one I'm working on lately, is to pass along that same kind of help to other people, people like your mother."

"But what if my Mom doesn't want to go? I'm pretty sure she wouldn't be interested in Alcoholics Anonymous."

"Then you—or you and your Dad together—have somehow got to *make* her go. You've got to tell her she's drinking too much, that you can't stand the smell, that you hate what she's doing to herself. You've got to convince her that AA is for those who can't be strong all by themselves."

"And if she still says no?"

"Well, you tell me you've tried everything to help her, Heather. Maybe you'll have to try the hardest thing of all—turning your back on her. You'll just have to tell her you're through helping her cover up, and that you're going on with your life until she herself sees the truth about it."

It was hard for Heather that evening, talking it over with her father, but Dad agreed that it was time to act.

"Oh, Dad, it hurts so much," she told him.

"I know, Heather. Every time we love someone we take a little risk of being hurt or disappointed. But we remember how good a person she was before the drinking took over. With God's help—and ours —she can be that way again. Let's do it. Let's talk to her right now."

Heather's mother resisted at first. "Look, I've got work to do. Could we talk about this another time?"

"No, Anne," Dad said. "Right now. Tonight."

"Please, not with Heather here."

"I belong here, Mom. Your sickness has spread to all of us. I'm a part of it too."

"I thought you were on my side."

Dad broke in. "We're both on your side, Anne. But we're not on the side of this sickness that's trying to destroy you."

"Don't be ashamed, Mom. Lots of people have the same problem. And the scary part is, people die from it. I love you, and I don't want you to die."

"Don't you think I feel bad about it?" Mom asked. Her voice trembled. "I don't need other drinkers to make me feel bad. If it's repentance you want, you've got it. I do feel rotten about myself."

"Repentance isn't just feeling bad about something," Dad explained. "It's deciding to turn around and go in a new direction. These other alcoholics have felt the same pain and hopelessness that you have, so if you should start to waver, they'll come running. I'll go with you, Anne, at least until you get acquainted."

"And so will my teacher," Heather said.

"Your teacher?"

"He's an alcoholic, Mom. He wants to help."

"Your teacher—Mr. Chellberg—an alcoholic?"

Heather's mother looked stunned. There was a long silence. Mother slumped forward, a look of pain in her eyes. She brushed the hair back from her face.

"OK. Maybe it won't work, but I know I can't do it alone. I've tried, and I can't do it alone. Ask your teacher about the next meeting."

Heather picked her backpack off the desk and dug a slip of paper from the pocket.

"Here's his phone number, Mom. You ask him."

"OK. I'll call him tomorrow."

"No, Mother. Now."

Mother managed a shaky smile. "Bossy kid," she said gently. "You win, Heather. Now."

> Three times I besought the Lord about this, that it should leave me; but he said to me, "My grace is sufficient for you, for my power is made perfect in weakness."
> 2 Corinthians 12:8-9a

Be with all alcoholics in their times of trouble, Lord. I know now they can't be strong all by themselves. They need family. They need the help of other people who have had problems with drinking, but most of all they need you. Show us the right way to love all of them and to help them. Amen

Operation Big Switch

Why can't my parents ever say anything but no? Everything I want to do around here is against a rule. I sometimes think I'd like to trade places with my best friend. She really has it nice.

"Come into the house, Rachel. It's important," her mother called from the doorway.

"Now what?" Rachel wondered as she dawdled up to the house. It was too nice outdoors to hurry inside. Morning sunlight warmed her head, but a cool wind pushed against her back. She paused on the doormat to scrape off the sprinkling of tree seeds that clung to the cold dew on her bare feet.

"Come on, Rachel. You've got to get packing."

"Packing? Where are we going?"

"We're not. You are. You're going to Tanya's house until Tuesday."

"I am? Neat! We'll have lots of fun together."

"No, you've got it wrong. Tanya won't be there."

"No? Then why am I going to her house? Where will Tanya be?"

"She'll be here," her mother said.

"Mom, you're not making any sense."

Amusement showed in her mother's eyes. "Sylvia Duncan and I have a plan. The code name for it is 'Big Switch.' "

"Big Switch?"

"Yes. We're going to trade daughters for awhile."

"You are? How come?"

"Well, Rachel, lately I've been hearing the same complaints over and over. 'Why can't I have a brother and sisters like Tanya does?' or 'Tanya's mother never sets the time for her piano practice' or 'Tanya gets to stay up later' or 'Tanya can eat snacks in the living room.' Everything's perfect at Tanya's house. Right?"

"That's right, Mom, and she can just help herself to ice cream any time without asking." Rachel paused, then added firmly, "I'm not at all sure she'd care to change places."

"Well, according to Sylvia, you're wrong about that. Tanya thinks it would be heaven to have her own room with a canopy bed. And she'd like to be an only child so she could have a bigger allowance and long vacation trips. She wouldn't have to wear Monica's hand-me-down clothes and she wouldn't have a brother like Tim breaking her crayons and bugging her all the time. Well, to make a long story short, Sylvia and I decided both of you deserved a little taste of paradise."

"Well, I guess it would work, except how would I

get to my piano lesson on Monday? And I think that's the day that Tanya baby-sits the neighbor's little boy while his mother works."

"No problem. It will be Sylvia's job to see that you get to your lesson, and you should be able to handle that sitting assignment."

Rachel hesitated a moment, then made up her mind. "Well, I guess it should be OK. Is this the day of the Big Switch?"

"That's right. But maybe I should add that we've set some ground rules."

Rachel frowned. "There had to be a catch somewhere," she said. "Well, OK. What are they?"

"The most important one is that neither of you will be treated like a royal guest. You'll be treated as a member of Tanya's family, and she'll be a member of ours. That means you eat what they eat, you follow the rules that they have, and if it's Tanya's turn to take out the garbage, that means it's your turn. No special treatment. OK?"

"OK."

"The switch is for five days—no more, no less. During those days you won't be allowed to see each other, but Sunday night you may talk it over in one of your marathon telephone conversations. Oh, and one more thing. We did agree that at the end of the experiment each of us would have to take her own kid back."

Rachel laughed. "Oh, Mom, you really are something."

"Well, honey, we're not sure how this will all turn out, but it'll be fun to try."

Rachel stacked clothes on the bed and watched as her mother refolded them and put them in her suitcase. Mom had said she should do it herself, but she usually changed her mind when she saw Rachel wasn't doing it right.

By this time Rachel was bubbling with excitement. "I'll bet I get to take care of Corky. You know I told Tanya once that I wished I had a baby sister, and she kind of groaned and said to me, 'You can have mine.' Tanya says she cries a lot, but I hold her sometimes when I'm over there, and I just love her. Maybe I'm just good with babies."

Minutes later Rachel saw Tanya's suitcase being carried up the driveway into her house while her own was being stowed into the Duncans' van.

"Good luck with Mother's rules, Tan," Rachel said in a half-whisper as she climbed into the van. "If you clip your fingernails in the living room, be sure to catch them in the ashtray or something. She goes crazy if they get sprinkled all over the carpet."

Tanya nodded. "Got it," she said.

A few minutes later, Rachel stood with Sylvia in the room Tanya shared with her big sister, Monica. "There should be room for your things at Tanya's end of the closet pole," Sylvia said. "Monica might get upset with you if you use her side."

Rachel noted silently that Monica's side was at least two-thirds of the pole. Luckily she hadn't brought too many clothes along. Then she looked around the room at the stereo components, the posters on the wall, the piles of records, and the clutter of mascara and shampoo bottles and lip slickers on the dresser.

"Better not mess with Monica's stuff," she said to herself. She knew that Tanya and Monica got into some fights about that.

Well, the sound of this house was certainly different from her own. Tim had TV blaring in the living room to drown out the sound of the news on his mother's kitchen radio. If anyone had anything to say to anyone else they just yelled—from one room to another, outside to inside, upstairs to downstairs. The house was never quiet.

"Rachel," Sylvia called to her from downstairs, "I think I hear Corky crying in her room. Her nap time is over. Why don't you change her diaper and then bring her down? The changing table is right beside her crib."

Changing? When Rachel had thought about Corky, it was playing and cuddling she had in mind. "Well, I guess it's part of the bargain," she thought.

As Rachel let down the side of the crib and awkwardly scooped the crying baby into her arms, Corky snuggled up to her, warm and pink-cheeked—and soaking wet.

Rachel dumped her on the padded table and held her down with one hand while she used the other one to fish for a disposable diaper from the stack. First the diaper and then the other clothes. She had watched Tanya do this a couple of times. She knew about the tapes for fastening it, but did Corky always wriggle like a fish in the bottom of a boat?

As Rachel stooped a little to put the wet diaper into the plastic can, Corky almost fell off the table. Rachel felt herself trembling with fear and—yes, with anger. Why couldn't Corky just lie still for one minute? Rachel again put the dry diaper under the squirming baby and tried to start over, but it was no use. It was impossible.

"Having trouble?" Monica asked from the door-

103

way. She was smiling, but it didn't seem funny to Rachel. "Give her something to hold, so she forgets about trying to escape," Monica suggested.

Rachel looked around for something, then in desperation handed Corky a little jar of baby cream. The baby began to examine it with wide-eyed calm. Her legs stopped pumping, and in no time Rachel had her dressed in clean, dry clothes.

Tanya had been right. Corky did cry a lot. When she was hungry she cried, when she was sleepy she cried, and she even cried about dumb things like when Sylvia spilled a little talcum powder on her sucking thumb.

That evening Rachel stood in front of the bathroom mirror, brushing her hair, slowly stroking back and upward, rolling the brush with each stroke.

"Mom," Tim complained at the top of his voice, "tell Rachel to brush her hair someplace else. I guess she doesn't know that in this house there is only one bathroom. Besides, I've got Little League."

"That's right, Rachel," Sylvia said briskly. "Get a move on. When there's a game, everybody goes."

Didn't it ever settle down around this house? Did everybody have to do everything together? Getting everybody out and into the van was like putting together an Antarctic expedition. With bigger families, going places got to be pretty complicated.

Rachel also discovered that having brothers or sisters meant having to take turns. It wasn't too bad having to wait for the bathroom or to take turns at reading the comics or clearing the table, but she was really surprised when she heard Tanya's father tell Tim he wouldn't be able to go to baseball camp next year because Tanya needed braces on her teeth.

At her house money had never seemed important. She had always had the comfortable feeling that if she really wanted or needed something, it was there. Why should Tim have to miss out on camp just because Tanya had to have braces? It didn't seem fair.

Sylvia Duncan was a nice lady, but she didn't seem to have much time to help Rachel. Like Saturday night, for example, when Rachel said, "Guess I didn't bring along enough clothes. Do you suppose you could wash a couple of things for me?"

"Well, Rachel," Sylvia said, "our two big wash-days are Wednesdays and Saturdays, and I don't provide service in between, but if the kids need something between times, they take care of it themselves. Just push the button that says 'Small Load.'"

Just push the button that says "Small Load"? There had to be more to it than that. Mom did things with water conditioners and detergent and stuff. Well, she needed clean socks, so the only thing to do was to go down there and read the dials and measure out detergent and take her chances. Actually, it worked out better than she expected.

Sunday after church Rachel sat on the back steps husking corn for the Duncan family's Sunday dinner. She didn't mind the job, ripping the crisp leaves back from the ears, pulling off the brown matted silk at the top, picking off the yellow strands that clung to the cool ridges of kernels. It was nice sitting there alone after the hubbub of leaving church —waiting for Monica to get her choir robe hung up and pulling Tim away from the pop machine and getting Corky out of the nursery.

Sitting there on the sunny steps, she got to thinking about her Mom and Dad. It seemed like weeks
ago that she had complained to Tanya, "My folks
don't talk with me. They make speeches. Everything
I do all day is going to affect my character. Makes
me feel like some government project instead of like
a kid."

Funny thing, but right now she missed home,
speeches and all. She missed the wind chimes outside her bedroom window. She missed standing by
the open bathroom door and watching her Dad cut
a clean swath through the shaving lather with his
blade. She felt like just walking down by the pond
with a brown bag of popcorn and feeding the ducks,
only there was no pond here and she couldn't see
any ducks.

A few hours later it was Tanya who put in the
promised Sunday night phone call. Right away Rachel noticed something different in her voice.

"You OK, Tan?"

"Sure, fine."

"Do you feel like a member of my family by now?"

"Well—"

"I know. We're both supposed to be just natural,
but it's hard, isn't it? It's supposed to be home, but
it isn't exactly."

"That's right, Rachel. When I used to visit your
house for awhile I guess I was being kind of polite,
but it's sort of hard to be polite for very long at a
time. Your folks start talking about relatives I don't
even know, and then they get all worried that I'm
feeling left out, so they ask me a real serious question. I feel like I'm being interviewed on TV or
something."

107

"You know what, Tan? I think Fritzie is worried about you. He sniffs your things in the closet and kind of whines, and he always sleeps at the foot of your bed."

"I know. It feels funny not having him tag me all over. I always thought it would be neat to have a kitten like Shadow to hold, but I never thought about having to clean the litter box. I don't mind taking my turn at jobs, but now when I'm the only kid it's always my turn."

"It's kind of neat at your house the way I don't have to eat things unless I want to," Rachel confided. "How do you like Mom's two-bite rule?"

"I'm not quite used to it yet. Yesterday I managed two bites of rutabagas, but I didn't ask for any more. Seems like your Mom doesn't think much of desserts, does she, Rachel?"

"Guess not. Just apples. My folks are both very big on apples, Tan. They worry about cavities."

"Yes. Well, I never did like apples." She paused. "Rachel, how come your mother puts oatmeal in chocolate chip cookies?"

"No special reason, I guess. It's just the recipe. I think maybe the oatmeal is good for you." She felt herself getting a little edgy at the question. This conversation was beginning to sound like a complaint list. "Hey, Tanya, have you been marking stuff down? I'm having to get used to some things, too, you know—like Corky's crying. You should have heard her when your Mom washed her scrungy old blanket. She hollered for half the morning. It didn't smell right to her or something."

"Well, she is just a baby, you know," Tanya snapped. "What do you expect?"

"Maybe a little peace and quiet once in awhile."

"Well, there's plenty of quiet around here—too much. Last night before dinner your folks went to the drugstore for a few minutes, and I was all alone in the house. I mean really alone. I'm not used to that. It was almost scary. Right about then I would have been relieved to hear the baby crying and Tim screaming and Fritzie barking."

Rachel couldn't take it anymore. "Isn't there anything right about my house? OK, so it isn't perfect. Maybe yours isn't either. Gotta go now, Tanya. Good-bye."

Rachel slammed down the receiver. "Well, Rachel, now you've done it," she thought. How could she tell Sylvia Duncan that she was tired of the experiment? How could she admit she was sort of homesick? How could she let her folks know she wanted it to be over? Switching houses had seemed like such a good deal, but the whole thing had wrecked a really good friendship.

Just then the phone rang again, and Rachel picked it up.

"Hi." It was Tanya's voice.

"Hi," Rachel answered, relieved.

"Would you say that the Big Switch was a big flop?"

"Well, kinda. Although I did find out coveting somebody else's house is a dumb idea. I always thought everybody else's home was a better deal than mine, but there I was sticking up for it."

"I know," Tanya chuckled. "I've decided there's not just a right way and a wrong way to do things. We're just used to it a certain way. Like the oatmeal

109

your Mom puts in the cookies. It's not really wrong, I'm just not used to it. Well, what do we do next?"

"Do? Well, I guess a bargain is a bargain, so we stick it out 'til Tuesday. And Tanya—"

"Yes?"

"Let's not tell our mothers we got mad. OK?"

"OK, Rachel. I can't stand it when anyone says 'I told you so.' "

"See you Tuesday, Tan."

"See you Tuesday."

> You shall not covet your neighbor's house.
>
> Exodus 20:17a

Lord, you've put me in a family, a good family, but not a perfect one. Sometimes I get the feeling that somebody has a better deal, but remind me that nobody's family is perfect and that this is the home in which you want me to live and to be happy. Amen